HOW IT LOOKS FROM HERE

Poetry from the Plains

Infusionmedia
Lincoln, Nebraska

© 2019 Nebraska Writers Guild

All rights reserved. No part of this publication may be used or reproduced in any manner without prior written permission, except in the case of brief quotations in critical reviews and certain other noncommercial uses permitted by copyright law.

Infusionmedia
2124 Y St, Flat #138
Lincoln, NE 68503
https://infusion.media

Printed in the United States of America

ISBN 978-1-945834-12-7 (paperback)
ISBN 978-1-945834-13-4 (ebook)

Library of Congress Control Number: 2019913377

Interior design and typesetting by Infusionmedia
Cover design by Kenneth Ryan V. Monteclaro at 99Designs

Contents

vii   *Foreword*

1   *Gone* Brad Anderson
3   *The Creation of Birds* Lucy Adkins
5   *Getting It Right* Lucy Adkins
7   *How the Culture Crumbled* Wayne Anson
8   *Trusting in a Lie* Dan Bean
10   *Church Ladies* Kristin Burnett
12   *The Progression of Trees* Kathleen Cain
14   *Bomb Cyclone* Kathleen Cain
16   *Open Water* Kathleen Cain
18   *Headstone Lost* Lynn Chelewski
20   *Night Approaches* Christine Egger
21   *Ironing* Rebecca Faber
23   *Tromso, Norway* Rebecca Faber
25   *Forty Days* Rebecca Faber
27   *That Day at Whole Foods in Which I Put Myself Back Together* Stephanie Fosbinder
30   *Torrent* Stephanie Fosbinder
32   *When the Night Cracks into a Fine Inaction* Stephanie Fosbinder
34   *In the After* Stephanie Fosbinder
36   *To the parents who sat behind me at my daughter's choir camp concert* Stephanie Fosbinder
40   *The Last Mile* Pat Frolander
41   *Our Sea of Tranquility* Pat Frolander
42   *The Dressmaker's Fingers* Julie Haase
43   *Aloft* Kathy Jacobs

45	*Tree of Knowledge*	Kathy Jacobs
48	*Loose Change*	Kathy Jacobs
51	*Em Counts*	Lori Joseph
52	*The Meadowlark Sings*	Lori Joseph
54	*Unfinished Dream*	Lori Joseph
56	*Threshold*	Lori Joseph
57	*Nebraskans*	James Luebbe
59	*My Neighbor's Barn*	James Luebbe
60	*Pretty Bird*	James Luebbe
62	*Overcross*	James Luebbe
63	*The Cure*	James Luebbe
65	*Things My Grandfather Left Me*	James Luebbe
67	*Tanzanian Bird*	Lynda Madison
68	*Midnight on the Inca Trail*	Lynda Madison
70	*Platte River Sandbar*	Lynda Madison
71	*Gravity*	Jill Marcusse
73	*Canning Peaches*	Jill Marcusse
74	*Broadway and 9th*	Ricardo Moran
77	*How to Create a Poet*	Charlene Neely
79	*Making Her Mark*	Charlene Neely
81	*What Stuart Left Out*	Charlene Neely
83	*In Your Shadow*	Charlene Pierce
85	*My One and Only*	Charlene Pierce
87	*Evolution*	Brandy Prettyman
89	*The Ballad of Rosie O'Grady*	Michael R. Ritt
93	*The Coal Miner's Life*	Michael R. Ritt
95	*The Perfect Rose*	Michael R. Ritt
98	*Chasing Wheat*	Steve Rose
100	*The brood cows*	Steve Rose
102	*If New Information Won't Stick*	Marge Saiser
103	*Looking for America*	Marge Saiser

105 *Our Windows Were Single Pane* Marge Saiser
106 *The Boogeyman* Maria I. Sanderson
108 *Looking Cool in School* Janet Sobczyk
110 *If I Must Go* Valerie Lee Vierk

113 Acknowledgments
115 Index by Author
117 Index by Title

Foreword

As the current publications chair for the Nebraska Writers Guild, I am proud to be part of the team bringing you the first poetry chapbook compiled by the NWG. While we are the *Nebraska* Writers Guild, our membership stretches as far north as Alaska, as far south as Texas, and from California to South Carolina. As expected, most of the poets in this chapbook are from Nebraska, but you'll also find poets from nine other states within these pages. Most of our poets are members; some are not (yet!). Our membership and diversity continue to grow, in part thanks to NWG-sponsored publications like this one.

In the past few years, the Nebraska Writers Guild has made the commitment to provide not only a supportive community for Nebraska writers but also a vehicle for putting their work out into the world. With this goal in mind, the Guild published its first anthology of short-form creative writing, *Voices from the Plains,* in 2017 and followed it in 2018 with *Voices from the Plains,* second edition. *How it Looks from Here: Poetry from the Plains* is the third compilation from the Guild (the first exclusive to poetry), and many more of its kind are planned in the years to come.

When we think of creative writing, we most often gravitate toward novels and short stories, humor, and children's books. Poetry, unfortunately, tends to linger back in the shadows, often forgotten and overlooked. Perhaps that is because poetry, more so than any other style of writing, is an art form that must be carefully considered and even studied. It's something a lot of people just don't get. Poetry challenges our perceptions and forces us to think about the world and who we are within it in new, unusual, and often provocative ways.

Poets don't simply entertain. They stimulate the senses and awaken the imagination, and they do so using far fewer words than any other writer could. With painstakingly selected language arranged just so and perhaps a sprinkling of rhythm and rhyme, poets take us places we've only dreamed about and evoke emotions we never saw coming.

For myself, I've written exactly one good poem (because it's hard!), and I could not be prouder that it has been selected to appear within these pages. To be considered worthy of this honor and to appear alongside the other remarkable, and certainly more talented, poets in this book is a thrill for me, and I'll be bragging about it for a good long time.

I hope you enjoy reading the poems offered herein. Perhaps you will laugh or cry or swoon. Perhaps you will be caught off guard, left to your thoughts, questioning what you thought you knew. Perhaps you will learn something about yourself. However these poems touch you, I have no doubt you will be better for the time spent with them. Happy reading.

Julie Haase
Publications Chair
Nebraska Writers Guild

Gone

Brad Anderson
Lincoln, NE

Gone...

Children at their desks
brilliant lives just beginning
before the school day ended
they were gone...

The faithful on their knees
find themselves in holy audience
before their worship ended
they were gone...

Each time restless did I sleep
did I know, could I feel
the souls of the dead
as they moved on?

Concert goers by the stage
Came with friends to sing and play

before the music faded
they were gone...

I weep for us all
grown used to the news.
We eat dinner, and count the toll
they are gone.

Commuters on a train
off to work to pay the rent
before the work day started
they were gone...

Who has the right
to steal a future
to take a life?
Where is our outrage?

...gone

The Creation of Birds

Lucy Adkins
Lincoln, NE

There must have been
an emptiness looking up,

a morning silence save
for a soughing of wind,

and that would have been
a sadness not to be borne.

For the world must be more
and the sky must be more

even with sunrises and sunsets
and a moon that walks the night.

But then there was the thought
like a leaf falling, but not falling,

the idea of a sky alive, curving
and warbling and winging,

directing the soul up.
That was the fifth day

when winged creatures came
to be upon the earth.

Getting It Right

Lucy Adkins
Lincoln, NE

There are times you manage to get it right,
little things like coffee measured, eggs fried,
bacon browned to its ultimate crispness,
all on the table on time and in style.

Sometimes the roses bloom just as the baby's breath
breaks out its arrows of light around each blossom;
and it stops you on the way to the compost pile
how god-awful beautiful this earth can be.

There are days the wind blows just a little,
stirs the yellow-green of the Kentucky Coffee Tree
into edgings of lace, and you've just moved
your chair to the right angle to see.

Or you persuade yourself there is bedlam
and woe on every floor of your castle,
then a poem flies off the printer
and knocks a little sense into you.

And maybe, your father calls, wants you to come,
but there is work, and time lost and distance, so you
say no. Then you call back and say yes, and that is
the last call, the last drive, the last visit, a time
you manage, for once and thank God, to get it right.

How the Culture Crumbled

Wayne Anson
Grand Island, NE

Steady dripping on the stone
Etched a hollow
Discovered a crack
Glossed it over
Until, untreated,
A winter frost
Cracked it open
And the culture crumbled.

Trusting in a Lie

Dan Bean
Crawford, NE

Greatness isn't given, honor is earned.
Peolple of the tribes lived as they learned.
Boldness was a trait, caution with every step.
Change coming about and death as they wept.
Navajo, Blackfoot, Lakota, to name a few,
these nations had their beliefs, and their point of view.

Cheyenne, Nez Perce, Mandan, Sioux,
At first helped the white man in what he wanted to do.
Indians lived off their lands, they treated with respect.
Things changed as the white man, from east to west,
He crept.

Arapaho, Chippewa, Apache don't understand.
Red Cloud, Crazy Horse say this is our land.
The blue coats say stay and you will die,
That's the only thing they were truthful about,
Everything else was a lie.

Black Kettle was a chief who trusted in their words,
They gave up their weapons, and gunshots were all they heard.
It didn't pay to trust them, they do nothing but lie,
Take away our freedom, give us blankets and we die.
You steal all the truth, and take away our land,
Telling all that we are savages and giving us that brand.

The white man wanted treaties, that he would always break,
killing, stealing, lying for their own sake.
Chief Joseph loved his people, and tried every endeavor,
giving them his promise, "I will fight no more forever."

These honorable people and chiefs of many tribes,
Trusted and believed in all the white man's lies.
You can take all we have and make us sick inside,
You think you have got it all, but you'll
Never get our pride.

Church Ladies

Kristin Burnett
Riley, KS

The building wasn't showy; but, it was
good. Sturdy. Clean.
Just so, it was God's House, and
we were embraced by Him in there,
filled with the joy of worship and
fortified to face another day.
It was that basement, though, where
God just made sure you understood
the point. He lived there.
Specifically, in the kitchen,
sardine-packed with women who stood
on and in between the points
of sinner and saint. Meek and mighty ladies
who taught Sunday School and sang in the
choir as easily as they fried chicken and
dished up scalloped potatoes and Jell-O
with arms steel-strong
from years of helping their parents and
farmer-husbands and
tending their own little flocks.

Those fleshy arms would grab us up—
and tight—
and we knew we were loved.

The Progression of Trees

after Hal Borland

Kathleen Cain
Arvada, CO

Jurassic. Begin with the cycads
(or maybe the gingko, we're still
not sure). And then the sago palm,
no palm at all, though spread into
four native species. Next, the conifers,
those cool pines and their kin
tucking life into cones that swing
with Fibonacci's rhythm. Keeping it
large, keeping it small. Among them,
the tamarack decides to shed its leaves,
like so many yet to come. The catkin-
bearers arrive: willows, poplars,
birches. One sex or two, sometimes
on the same tree. Pollen or seeds,
not all that big a leap from the cone.
But, oh, those leaves, shedding year
after year, into millennia. And then,
the succession across time. The flower-
bearers arrive. Microscopic at first.
On the maple, only a matter of stamen

and pistil. Still. Oaks. Hickories.
Lindens. Look out! Here comes
the rose family. "An apple, a plum,
a pear, a cherry." 100 million years
ago. Tertiary. Here. Waiting for us.

Bomb Cyclone

for PD

Kathleen Cain
Arvada, CO

Some doubt the bombogenesis,
Consider it pretentious,
But NOAA has it well defined
This land-cyclone contentious.
It broke the charts at DIA
With wind speeds over eighty.
Stirred floods and ice jams all the way
Down river roads to Big Muddy.

It's not just about the snow, you see,
But temperature and blizzard:
The wind sustained at thirty-five
Three hours or more; a dither
Of gusts and drifts, all blinding.
And then there is the pressure drop;
Barometric formula most binding.
The millibars, down twenty-four,
In the same number of hours.

For model, watch how water swirls
Down sink or commode, in spiral.
How like the eye of hurricane
Or black hole, going viral.

Except the wheel of swinging snow
Will change to water storm.
If you doubt it, just ask Nebraskans
Still searching for the shore.

Open Water
for JH

Kathleen Cain
Arvada, CO

"How does an atheist pray?" he asked
when I told him of another human need
among those we know. I didn't have
an answer, except to say I wasn't sure.
On second thought, I told him: "maybe it's
a matter of good intentions."

Do you need a god to wish another well?

Trumpeter swans need open water to feed,
but when they arrive in winter to find the lake
frozen over, they sleep on the ice, tucking
their long necks into their wings. They
rest until the wind rises, or the sun, carrying
the scent of water. Or until they remember
the way to another lake along the route.

Then, some signal passed between them,
they stretch their long precious bodies
into the sky, until you can see, clearly,

the black bills and legs, and the way
they elaborate the air. If you're
lucky, maybe you'll hear them.
Maybe it's like that.

Headstone Lost

Lynn Chelewski
Beatrice, NE

Beneath a quagmire of golden corn,
Fanny, poor lass,
Lies forgotten,
Forlorn.
She passed away
on the Mormon Trail.
An insidious illness
Became her fate.
It was back in 1867,
When Nebraska became a state.
Near the Platte River,
She lies on the plains,
No longer a stone,
To mark her remains.
"Progress" cleared the grove of trees
Where her body was laid to rest,
And the weed shrouded limestone marker
Put up but a feeble protest.
Was a child when I saw it in '67.

I remember the simple, crude carving,
"Fanny 1867"

Night Approaches

Christine Egger
Stratton, NE

Indigo blue, gold and rose
Splattered across the sky,
Sun dives toward the mountains,
Shadows lengthen
Creeping across the land,
Creatures of the night appear
Coyote loping across the pasture,
Owls swooping down on unsuspecting prey,
Sun completes its arc,
Darkness prevails,
Stars twinkle coldly in the velvet sky
The night is silent and still.

Ironing

Rebecca Faber
Lincoln, NE

You want what I want, by our own definitions.
—Rex Walton

In high school, I owned three skirts—
one to wear on Monday and Wednesday,
one for Tuesday and Thursday,
and the black one I wore on Fridays.

To maintain this schedule, I had to iron. Every night.
The wrinkles must come out, the fabric must appear to
   be fresh,
nothing puckered,
every pleat flat.

This is how I have approached your shirts,
pulled tightly over the ironing board,
heat and steam at my command,
each shoulder well pressed,
each sleeve without wrinkle,
each minute at the ironing board just one of my ways

to make things right.
You want what I want—that you will appear perfect.

My ways are women's ways, although I do not know who now
is ironing your shirts,
what practice those hands have in smoothing
and pressing
and caring.

With only three skirts, I learned that to do something over and over
is to learn the pace of a life,
a pace that laid itself out
while I stood in one spot,
with heat and steam,
with innocence and youth.

Tromso, Norway

Prompted by Mark Rothko's Yellow Band

Rebecca Faber
Lincoln, NE

North of the Arctic Circle
dark rules entirely from the end of November
to late January

so we drink,
eat fish and potatoes,
then drink some more

and wonder why we live here
in this space beyond humanity,
why we bring babies into this world
of madness and suicide,
of nights/days too long to bear
followed by days/nights
of unending sun.

We dream of a place
where moderation rules,
where a band of yellow

appears early in the morning
and again late in the afternoon.

How are we to teach our children
to reach for the stars
when we cannot tell
day
from
night?

Forty Days

Rebecca Faber
Lincoln, NE

Their scripture states that the soul
does not depart the body
until 40 days
after death

Then their grief begins
as they mourn the spirit

What is not in the scripture
is that the soul prepares
for 40 days
prior to death—

those soon to depart
feeling a pressure on the heart,
attacks of nostalgia,
the sound of fluttering in quiet moments,
their hands unable to remain still

The soul breaks cocoon,
Death's butterfly evolving

That Day at Whole Foods in Which I Put Myself Back Together

Stephanie Fosbinder
Gretna, NE

When I saw him in the produce
section at Whole Foods on that Sunday
afternoon, I was surprised

because he looked
as if he were trying to decide
between plain and flavored

hummus. I was surprised
because he had never been
a hummus kind of guy. Though
he didn't have

much flavor either.

He saw me, then glanced away
and back again. He put both
in his cart—does he have

flavor now, perhaps—and he said
hey. Hi, I said, smiling and maintaining
eye contact, but being profoundly more

focused
(lie) on adjusting the strap of my
shoulder bag and then pulling

out my phone just to have
something
on which to hang.

How have you been? he asked
innocently, as if we were
old high school friends who hadn't

been in touch since our 10-year
reunion, or maybe it was
15? Good, I said

as he prattled on about his new sales job
selling—cars or clothes or electronics
or futures—I cannot recall, but

he must be good. He always sold

me on his lies. You look good
(lie), he said and I said I was good
(lie), and I said I was writing
(lie), and I said I was back in town
and I said I was all better now

(lie). Don't I seem
better? He looked
through me then, not into

my eyes but through and
said he always knew
I would be.

Torrent

Stephanie Fosbinder
Gretna, NE

I know how Sisyphus feels. The never-
ending boulder battle, constantly obeying
gravity. My size considerably

smaller than his. My insurmountable
obstacle wet and hollow. My climb
vertical, a tunnel straight

up to the heavens. My arduous journey begins
anew. My belief strong, the finish
line seen with all eight eyes. My faith guides

me like echolocation. I will
make it. This is the moment
in which I triumph. The elusive

success. Alas, it is not to be. The deluge
comes again. Drown in failure.
And repeat.

Repeat.

I reach
for purchase, straining all
eight legs, but the whirlpool
vortex
swirls
me
down
until once again I am

vomited onto the asphalt, ripped from my
aspiration. I scuttle from the shallow pavement
pool. Water flows with no regard. It cares
not for my failure. Nor
my success.

And again, I delight in the rays
of the sun, as they point
me back
into the maw.

When the Night Cracks into a Fine Inaction

Stephanie Fosbinder
Gretna, NE

The gunfire splinters
the night, cracks
through the edge of music.
A new playlist, this soundtrack of
death. The crowd hesitates,
disbelief surrounds, then
injuries and death abound,
To those just out
for a night of
Life. Not again.
Not. Again.
Here, the silence overwhelms.

But, oh, the bravery
so many wore, alongside
their cowboy hats and festival
bands. Heroes jump into the
fray, create
shields from skin
and muscle, from fabric

and prayer. They eat
their fear, spit
out their anger like bones,
which later turn to ash
in the desert sun.

Again, we ask: What will stop
the next bullet barrage? We look
to those who (claim to) lead, but
find no answers, as
thoughts and prayers
are a fine inaction.
Comfort found
only in the maybe, the
maybe that this is the one
which reaches into
the mouths of America, and
pulls out the discussion.

In the After

Stephanie Fosbinder
Gretna, NE

After the baby
died, I built
a life of alcohol,
walls bricked in bars of Xanax.
Anything to obliterate
the empty-arm ache, to
anesthetize
the empty-crib devastation.
I made never-worn baby socks
my worry stone, rubbing
at the tiny cuff penguin, an attempt
to magic my baby back to life.

After the doctor said
"I'm sorry" and
"We did everything we could,"
my life fractured
into the before,
and the after.
Each fresh day,

for the slightest time
sliver, I am whole,
until
the tsunami of
pain, until
I reach for the numb
to deaden my day away.
To feel only
the dead that is my baby.

To the parents who sat behind me at my daughter's choir camp concert

Stephanie Fosbinder
Gretna, NE

You thought it was a good thing, bringing
young kids to hear their sister sing. You know
how hard she worked
this past week. You do know,
right? In a mere
five-and-a-half days, the choir learned
eight
full
songs—one in Latin, which
no one even speaks anymore—
But they learned eight songs (including the one in Latin)
and performed them all beautifully. I mean,
I guess they did. Perhaps,
if you would have kept your kids quiet,
I would know they did. Perhaps,
if you would have chosen a place to sit knowing
that young children do not sit well. Perhaps,
if you knew that young children who do not sit well
may disturb others. Perhaps,
if you would have told your son to stop

sticking
his foot in the air
adjusting
his sock, to put
his shoes back
on, and for the love of
all that is holy, stop
kicking the seat. Because
1—
    2—
        3—
seats to his right, one row up was
me. And I could not
enjoy Land of the Silver Birch or Something Told the
    Wild Geese or
even Hey! Diddle Diddle without
being
jostled
by your son. Kicking
the seat. Four seats and one
row away. You never
once told him to stop. Oh, right,
you didn't notice.
Your daughter,
no little saint herself,
kept standing up, flipping
her hair around, moving from lap
to lap. And lap
to lap. And seat
to lap.
Again.

Speaking. Speaking
again. Not loudly, but
no whisper. You did not tell her to sit
down and be quiet. You did not tell her
we are here to listen. You did not tell
her to be still and listen and appreciate the hard
work her sister put in this week on these
eight
(brand new to them—and yes one in Latin!)
beautiful songs. But, why
would you? You
(must never have been taught to listen)
couldn't keep your mouths closed either. Maybe your
    daughter, the one
singing her heart
out
on stage, the one who
was
maybe
standing
next to
mine, the one whose
family sat in the second row, bringing her great joy
at first, until she noticed
their disruption.
The one whose
voice
became
smaller and
smaller with
each song, because

why not? No one was there to listen to her sing her
eight-just-learned-and-one-is-in-Latin songs. And so,
the son kicked
and
the daughter flipped
and
the parents stared
(at their phones, of course)
and I turned and
I glared.
And
the older daughter, who had started the day
bright,
slowly dimmed
dimmed
dimmed
                                      until there was no
              Light
     At
All.

The Last Mile

Pat Frolander
Sundance, WY

Thirty-one miles of county road,
eleven ranches, eight widows—

Three never kept a checkbook.
Two never set foot in barn or field.
One lost the land to repossession.
One survived on charity of neighbors.

The last one, my friend, couldn't take it anymore.

Our Sea of Tranquility

Pat Frolander
Sundance, WY

Feather clouds laze across the cornflower blue.
Walleye, bass, and crappies slumber in sun-warmed
    waters.
Bobbers ripple on soft waves drifting toward the dam.
We cat-nap, soaking in the heat, arming ourselves for
    winter.

Even the flies are languid, their drowsy buzz adds
to the rhythm of slumber.
This is a special day, two of us craving the slow slap
    of water,
the laziness of it all . . . and somewhere deep in my bones
I know
this day shall not come again.

The Dressmaker's Fingers

Julie Haase
Omaha, NE

caress the satin fabric, white and crisp,
which cascades from her lap in creamy folds.
The needle, as a natural extension
of her fingertips, directs the thread in its course.
The bodice envelopes the mannequin with sleeves
of ivory satin tapering into lacey wrists.
Embroidered collar gently hugs the neckline.
The detail of the stitches comes together
in a pattern, intricate and alluring,
creating forms like ornamental snowflakes.
She joins the skirt and bodice into one,
the sheer material reaches for the floor,
a pearlescent gown in honor of faith and love.
The dressmaker feels the fabric with satisfied hands.
Resting with weary eyes in sight of her creation,
she lays her hands in her lap. She sleeps.

Aloft

Kathy Jacobs
Lincoln, NE

The swan
   yes it must have been a swan because
I knew swans lived on this river
   and I know the shape of
herons in flight
   spindled legs long behind them
when the swan materialized
   far ahead of the bow
my breath caught
   as she canted and levered along the
imperceptible current
   body and wings arced into
an archer's bow
   a white so pure how I imagined
saints' robes to be
   suddenly her partner appeared
figures tethered by
   invisible thread, dipping sliding
growing smaller with the distance
   and my heart

wrecked by joy
   rang out
wait
   for me
wait for me

Tree of Knowledge

Kathy Jacobs
Lincoln, NE

Clearly your daughter has dyslexia
the psychologist told them
It's why she scores so
poorly on standardized tests
asks Little Sister to read
the bedtime stories aloud
But she is very bright he reassured
has adapted through memorization
guessing words in context
going through the same books
repeatedly
The teachers have not suspected
because she gets As
in her schoolwork
He showed them
a drawing of a house
A house he explained
represents how children
see their family life
Your daughter drew

a happy house
He pointed to
the open windows
big smiling sun
stick figures holding hands
The next drawing showed
a single tree
"The tree represents how
your daughter sees herself"
The tree was large
leafy green limbs emerged
from a sturdy brown trunk
with a black knothole
at the center
My tree is not perfect
she had told him
She sees herself as flawed
he said

When is a knothole
just a knothole
the mother thought
Nature being decorative
A nest for wood ducks
A cranny for nuts
In *To Kill a Mockingbird*
a knothole was a post office
linking an isolated soul
with some wise children
Not a missing piece
an aberration a gouge in

someone's portrait of perfection
It didn't *define* the tree
make it an ash
instead of a willow
When they got home she helped
her daughter tape the house
and the tree
to the refrigerator door
They would read a new book
without little sister
later

Loose Change

Kathy Jacobs
Lincoln, NE

life turns on a dime
one day you're merrily
spinning around
the next an anvil falls
on your head
you lie on the ground
stare at a fluorescent sky
and ask where did
that come from
you're shattered what
does it matter

you wonder if you
should bother getting up
in case there's another
anvil coming along
how can it hurt
any more than this
you're afraid it might

you realize your brokenness
is invisible to the hand
that dropped the anvil
it moved on without
bothering to wave
which makes the pain
grow worse

the anvil slides off your head
to sit on your chest
no one has noticed you lying there
perhaps no one has to know
how your thoughts were concussed
and your heart pumped out nothing

you think if
instead of spinning
you had been rolling
you wouldn't be
flattened so flat
which hardly matters when
your heart is pressed thin
so precariously thin
your fingernails can't slip underneath
no room to slide a single sheet of
love song or peace offering
or hate mail or farewell note

maybe that's what matters now
just thinking it might be possible
to lift your heart edge

you lie in silent watch
to learn if you're made of
some kind of metal

Em Counts

Lori Joseph
La Plata, MD

When I was a child
I would carry the bucket
twenty-seven steps to the well.
I would turn it over and stand upon it
to reach the pump handle.
Nine times I'd have to pump, to prime the flow.
It took two hands and a clenched jaw
to carry the sloshing weight.
As the years passed, my steps were fewer
and my clothes drier.
This is how I learned to count.

                                        Em

The Meadowlark Sings

Lori Joseph
La Plata, MD

It's ninety-four outside
and still as an empty rocking chair.
Mother insisted on visiting the old vacant homestead
to retrieve a memory or two.

I stamped down the weeds bursting with grasshoppers
to clear a path for her.
Holding my arm to steady herself,
she told me the boards above the porch,
the ones splayed like piano keys,
reminded her of the music, the dance and the laughter
that once shook the horsehair and lath.
On Saturday nights they'd open the door
and roll up the rugs to create a dance floor,
welcoming folks to celebrate life.

We stood for a reflective moment,
I felt her pat my hand,
she had relived enough and was ready to go.

The following evening and for many to come
I revisited the old vacant homestead
where the door's still open
and the meadowlark sings.

Unfinished Dream

Lori Joseph
La Plata, MD

Fifty-four years had passed since
he last took the switchback
leading to the old ranch.
He remembered riding standing up
in the bed of the truck wearing
his first pair of pint-size ropers
with no socks and carrying a pocket knife.

As he drew closer, the low rumble
of the diesel and scent of the sagebrush
gripped him. He pulled over
leaving the truck silent, loaded with lumber
and the door open. Inside, hanging from the rearview
mirror was a cross,
made of fool's gold,
sending prisms with the breeze.

Silas perched himself on the boulder.
Leaning back and crossing his feet
he fiddled with the season's blade of grass,

tasting it. His eyes fell into the shadow from the brim of his canted Stetson.
It was time to tend to his grandfather's unfinished dream.

Threshold

Lori Joseph
La Plata, MD

On the other side of the barbed wire fence
the horizon boasts a doorless entry.
All six-foot-two crawled in
from the prairie grass.
No hat, no boots, just she.
A sturdy pioneer who withstood
dustbowls and hailstorms,
crossing the plains.
Arriving parched and delirious,
unable to speak.
She and her story saddle the threshold.

Nebraskans

James Luebbe
Beaver Crossing, NE

First True Nebraskan,
the Ponca Chieftain declared
"I am a man," and interred
his Prairie Flower among the rolling hills,
flat waters, spirit-rich soil.
First Nebraskans too,
the driven Winnebago and Santee Sioux,
where the wide skies pour out our loss, the broken flint
and blood-tinted loess a trail of tears
hoof-pounded by the buffalo ghost millions,
scattered like the crane-thick clouds
of passenger pigeons, thinning monarch
sundrop migrations.
Spirit-filled prairie
teeming in new growth, new Nebraskans,
English, Swedes and Slavs,
Sudanese and Yazidis, gold still flying
on meadowlarks' wings, hillsides bright
with globemallow, leadplant, spiderwort and phlox,
all the dreamcatchers' prairie bloom

and cottonwood seed drifting by
on an Oglala chant that snags among pink penstemon
and grama grass, singing its new notes, birdsong on
the thousand-mile wind or Lakota drumbeat
booming in our chests, the echo of Standing Bear
closing a circle, calling the new tribes
to Nebraska.

My Neighbor's Barn

James Luebbe
Beaver Crossing, NE

Eyesore yes,
or fascinating spot to limber up a neck
lean against a pole   watch
a swallow arrow into place.
Pain in the neck to paint again.
A wild tree is plumb entangled
with one corner   the oddly angled roof
should be reshingled.
Won't be.
That weathered face, those mangled eaves,
might fool you that its owner
wants it down.
Don't be.

Pretty Bird

James Luebbe
Beaver Crossing, NE

Arnie Boldt would stroll across the stage
at the Goehner Melodrama between acts,
cane, vest, gartered sleeve and straw hat,
with first-time visitors, mouths full of popcorn,
waiting there to fly. The tinny tune
of the honky-tonk piano and Arnie
whistling *Bird in a Gilded Cage*,
warbling two notes at a time, clear,
golden, and swinging his cane,
a bright blizzard of songbirds
filling out sight. Meadowlarks and warblers,
cardinals and flickers feathering their paths
through those windbreaks now crowding
upward in the Grange Hall.
And above me, a watercolor swirl
of tropical parakeets caged in a tool shed,
and pale blue Pretty Bird who rode
Grandpa's shoulder out through the porch door,
freed up into the huge backyard catalpa.
The rest were turned loose to join him,

the Beaver Crossing sky broken apart but alive
in the cottonwoods all that summer.
The whistling of Arnie's pure notes,
darting above us all, the flights of our childhood
threatening to leave, more free than we dared,
those young notes recklessly circling
and when the winged doors of the Hall swing
open they fly us home, light, soaring,
Pretty Bird's flock back from the tropics,
trilling the losses from our lives.

Overcross

James Luebbe
Beaver Crossing, NE

His father's world; Paul has not made
all he sees, but has remade it
with the care of a solemn oath.
The machine shed is plain but neat,
the tools free of rust though not so new.
His tractors have been washed, the oil changed,
the loose corner of barn tin nailed down tight.
He spent the morning ordering his way
across the backlot, checking fences,
adding weight to the silage tarp,
and searching out what undone piece of worry
might undo his good work.
He drifts asleep, his breath
lined up to the cold blow coming
and hears a distant creak,
sealing his resolve to check once more
the bricks on that old chimney.

The Cure

James Luebbe
Beaver Crossing, NE

She sits with arms extended,
hands turned up, cupped,
keeping them in line
as if they would betray her.
She thinks she suffers for her sins
but cannot name them.
The raw eroding flesh is a fungus
or an eczema
or rawhide burns from branding cattle;
her doctors can't agree.
She takes their various cures
and adds her own.
Her body will not heal itself,
she thinks it would reject her,
would cast off her own opened hands
for some recent unnamed sin.
What sin? What sin?

She lies awake within the dark restrictions
of her room, her hands in layered creams,

no light there to reflect.
She's never liked herself, she thinks.
Her hands have found her out.
She hears the clock tick slowly on,
listens to the story being told,
and feels the vicious rumor
spreading toward her wrists.

Things My Grandfather Left Me

for George Mehuron

James Luebbe
Beaver Crossing, NE

A leather-wound, ivory-capped
       handmade walking stick.
That peanut butter wiped on bread
       is always called a "lick."

The joy of gadgets, toys that last.
Fast cars driven fast.

"To my old Pal," a racer inked
And smiled, before he went extinct.

A scoped bolt-action .22.
The Book of Wonders. Wanders. Blue.

The urge to tease, to make a joke.
Regrets of what went up in smoke.

The thrill of risks, of doing all.
A black and broken fortune ball;

"The signs say maybe," it must answer.
The fear of maybe getting cancer.

The fear of ever being poor.
Attention span that's much too shor–

Tanzanian Bird

Lynda Madison
Omaha, NE

To rise like the lilac breasted roller,
swoosh above the Rift valley,
the beige, open savannah,
vervets in trees, rock pythons below,
cheetahs and gazelles, all
tinted orange in the afternoon light;
if I were a lilac breasted roller,
I would not be bothered by a jeep
that tears up the grass, or dust
suspended in air. I would ascend,
donned in blue, pink, and yellow,
because I arrived that way, lay out
feathered wings with falcons and doves,
dive for lizards and snails to survive,
alight upright, somehow, without
pain or impalement, to perch again
among the thorns.

Midnight on the Inca Trail

Lynda Madison
Omaha, NE

Stars reflect sunlight from some ambiguous angle as I
crawl from my mountain tent, sit alone on the grass.
A paintbrush has been dipped in white, scraped across
the Andean sky.

No North Star orients my place; here,
in the lower half of the globe, the Southern Cross points
its longest arm toward dark silhouettes
amid the spattered stars of Willkamayu,

Incan Sacred River,
its wide expanse flowing toward the South Polar Pit.

I make out a serpent, partridge, toad, fox,
Yana Phuyu, Mother Llama: her head, her eyes,
her long black neck bent low to nuzzle
a smaller llama nearby.

It is Christmas in Nebraska, but here in summer
solstice, mother and child drink
from the waters of Willkamayu.

This is the consciousness of Zen,
space in the interval of form and not-form;
in Japan, *Ma*, the gaps
between structural parts,

the rests in a song
that give the whole its shape.

Electrons move inside me, and in the rock
that holds me up, each one dancing
in the space of an atom its own unique pattern,
some gentle like a waltz, others,
the wild Festejo.

How wide is the universe?
How infinitesimal
I was once told, were space removed
from any solid, all matter would compress
to nothingness,
to particles unseen.

Platte River Sandbar

Lynda Madison
Omaha, NE

Your edges light up first,
when the sun catches
a low angle, finds patterns
the water has worn, logs
that have drifted and stuck,
puddled tracks of turtles,
wood thrush and deer,
their small impressions,
your long expanse.

Gravity

Inspired by Dale Nichols' "Footsteps in the Snow"

Jill Marcusse
Grand Rapids, MI

A deep Midwestern winter,
snow blue as the sky above.
A man comes from the weathered
equipment shed, shovel in hand,
stands at the grain elevator's door.

His footsteps in the snow are the only
signs of stirring in the day so far.
Last night the wind blew round
the buildings, and the snow drifted,
filled the tire ruts in the yard,
curled round the stone foundations.

He steps inside the elevator:
its shafts and chutes, belts and levers,
wheels and gears all still. The lingering
chaff stirred up from the floorboards
floats in light like a cathedral's.

He leans the shovel against the wall,
climbs the narrow ladder between the bins
to the top. He can see ten miles to Falls City
where a cluster of grain silos dominates
the landscape like this elevator used to here.

Back in the day, he thinks. *Back before
the railroad pulled the spur. When
we loaded a hundred boxcars of wheat a year
When we felt the grain in our hands.
Obsolete. This elevator. Me.*

He looks down the shaft where gravity
pulled the grain, wonders what it would feel like
to let gravity have its way now. He turns,
grips the worn rungs of the ladder,
makes his slow descent.

Canning Peaches

Jill Marcusse
Grand Rapids, MI

The knife slipped easily in
      pulled the scalded flesh loose,
           found the stone, pirouetted.

Halved in my slippery hand
      into wide mouthed jars, I slid
           the peaches one upon the other.

Come morning,
      I too was split open,
           my daughter plucked from me

Caesarian. A perfect peach,
      unblemished, with sweetness
           clinging to her downy head.

Broadway and 9th

Ricardo Moran
San Diego, CA

As I stand on the corner of
Broadway and 9th
the spotlight rolls overhead.

The cast of clouds move
the audience, their shadows
welcomed for the performance.

My voice rises,
my hands lifted over the stage
of grass and goldenrod.

The crimson glow,
commences the 2nd half.

The lights of heaven turn on.
And I am finally
among the stars.

For I did not find them
on the sidewalks of
Hollywood.

I found them
in the criss-cross of wheat fields,
living in eaves, gables and doorways,
in abandoned schools, stores, and
churches
where spirits still chatter, sing, and
applaud.

I did not find the stars in
the tall concrete shadows,
in the crawling cars
on tangled asphalt suspended
over cardboard camps,
under the orange sky.

I found them at the intersection
of quilts of wheat,
in the tips
of bluestems and buffalo grass,
in the specks of dew drops.

I found the applause
in the curtains of trees
standing stoically,
promenading in place.

In the cornstalks stretching
their necks in the luminescence.
A captive audience
miles to the back row.

I did not find my voice
in Hollywood,
on the surface
of smoked glass
where everything lived.

Now when I sing,
the lines
on my face cut
sharply as the plow
on soft Nebraskan soil.

My eyes rest in the darkness,
my voice rises to the stars
as I stand on the corner
of Broadway and 9th.

How to Create a Poet

Charlene Neely
Lincoln, NE

Before you write a poem,
you have to create the poet to write it.
—Antonio Machado

Teach them to sit on a river bank
without a fishing pole to listen
to the stories the water has to tell.
Tell them to use their words,
their inside voices, and outside voices.

Teach them to sit at the back of the bus
studying the gentle ebb and flow
of the passengers as they come and go,
eavesdropping on their conversations.
Tell them not every poet
sounds like Shakespeare or Keats.

Teach them to spend hours
in a garden or forest absorbing

the light and sounds, imagining
the creatures that make them.
Give them dictionaries and
thesauruses for Christmas.
And a thousand little notebooks,
a number 2 pencil and a
pocketknife to keep it sharp.

Let them stew in their own pot
for days on end or go out
into the world to discover how
it creates itself new every day.
Do not tell them poets are sissies.
But slide some Kloefkorn into their
backpack when they aren't looking.

Tell them Poetry is the place
you can break all the rules,
so long as you know them first.
Tell them they can change the world.

Making Her Mark

Charlene Neely
Lincoln, NE

The row of calendars
went around three sides of the room,
marching in circles, marked
with neat, orderly X's
made with a pencil tied
to the nail holding

this year's seed corn issue
with its twelve pictures
of crops the like of which
would never thrive
on this God-forsaken land.

That is, all but the third
Wednesday of last March,
the day the old coot set out
to walk to town for a jug
of whiskey in the worst
storm anyone around recalled.

They found him
six days later, five days too late.
She'd marked that day in red—
blood from the finger
she'd nicked peeling potatoes
as the door slammed behind him.

And here it is November
and she was still
marking off the days.
Maybe when there were
no more days to mark off
she'd gather her few treasures—

the quilt her mother gave her,
her Sunday-go-to-meeting hat.
She'd set the caged canary free,
leave the un-used cradle in the corner.

Maybe she'd prick her finger
to make the final X,
after all weren't all the
good days marked in red.

What Stuart Left Out

Charlene Neely
Lincoln, NE

Tonight the moon has a street number...

That moon has taken up residence
on the roof top of 1624 Eighth Avenue,
been hanging around there for nights.

The photographer across the street
hasn't slept with his wife since
it showed up posing on the parapet
like a magician's ball on a string.

The poet who lives in the apartment
next to him stays up until the wee hours
filling her notebook with line after line.

While the old lady who lives below her
complains all day because its light
shines in her eyes and bounces
off the mirror beside her bed all night.

And Vinnie, the neighborhood thug,
and his pals have taken up praying
for rain as they shuffle between
the pool hall and shot-out street lights,
grumbling about poor working conditions,
unable to hit a target as big as the moon.

It will take more than a new day to erase tonight's moon.

*lines in italic are from *Seven Sentences* by Stuart Dybek

In Your Shadow

Charlene Pierce
Omaha, NE

Following your shadow,
trying to stretch big to fill
yours. Watching your confident
step. Memorizing
you. When strangers approached,
hiding in that safe
spot behind your right
leg, knee high.

Following your instructions
in the kitchen, watching
counter high, learning
how to make
from scratch.
A family
gathers round. You made
each their favorite
pie and rolls from dough, shaped,
pulled, kneaded, left to rise

under the safety
of your hands.

Now, I'm surrounded
in laughter of family,
head of the table. The warmth
from the kitchen oven seeping,
stretching its arms out covering
us. The scent of your favorite
pie filling us with memories
of you. And I stand tall, forever
in your shadow.

My One and Only

Charlene Pierce
Omaha, NE

When I was thin
I occupied the same skin.

Young and fast metabolism back then.

I didn't know, and I didn't understand, what size I was in
that I was thin.

I felt fat.
Society told me that.

My ribs pushed through my skin.
I felt plain.
The kids at school told me the same.

Looking back,
my high school photo, when I was thin
I think, maybe, I was pretty then.

Now youth is gone,
my metabolism slow

and I'm supposed to know
who I am in this skin.

I have lines around my eyes,
grey hair that I try to hide
to look younger than I am

not yet comfortable in this skin.

My belly is round
I think I've found
that it doesn't matter how pretty I am
in this skin.

It is the same skin
that I occupied when I was thin.

Evolution

Brandy Prettyman
Papillion, NE

Dust drifting within the beam of sunshine
Dancing, quiet, peaceful, still
Small particles of our home intertwine

The home we built, my location, your design
Our surprise getaway, the suspense, the thrill
Dust drifting within the beam of sunshine

Your framed print of the New York skyline
My Broadway swag, a cast-signed handbill
Small particles of our home intertwine

Business meetings that ran late, clandestine
Your gaze on the neighbor from our windowsill
Dust drifting within the beam of sunshine

The lipstick red on your collar, not mine
My hotel receipt from Charlottesville
Small particles of our home intertwine

Two children born—each form a new bloodline
The vows we spoke, unable to fulfill
Dust drifting within the beam of sunshine
Small particles of our home intertwine

The Ballad of Rosie O'Grady

Michael R. Ritt
Huson, MT

Rosie O'Grady
Was a dance hall lady.
She worked down at the Longbranch Saloon.
And every night
She would make quite a sight
As she danced and she sang out a tune.

With long hair flowing
(And some ankle showing)
The cowboys would all give a holler.
She'd peddle her wares
Then she'd take them upstairs
And it only cost them a dollar!

Late one November
As best I remember
The night of the local election,
A cowboy came in
And got loaded on gin
And demanded Rosie's affection.

This cowboy was tough
And got a little rough
And was slapping poor Rosie around.
She thought, "This ain't fun."
So she grabbed for a gun
And she fired and the cowboy went down.

The sheriff in town
Hadn't long been around,
They'd just put him in office that day.
He was far too new
And didn't know what to do,
So he went and locked Rosie away.

Though things had got tense
It was clear self-defense,
No one thought she would stay long in jail.
But the town saw its chance
Now to end Rosie's dance,
So Judge Parker refused to set bail.

The day of the trial
Rosie sat with a smile.
The courtroom was standing room only.
And most of the men
Had, a time and again,
Come to Rosie to feel less lonely.

The jury came in
And to Rosie's chagrin,
She saw and it caused her to worry,

The town had conspired
To have Rosie retired.
There wasn't a man on the jury!

Now Rosie could see,
It was plain as could be,
That her fate had already been sealed.
Without any hope
She would hang from a rope,
And the verdict could not be appealed.

The following day
They took Rosie away
To the gallows the townsmen had built.
And none of the guys
Could look her in the eyes
Because every man there felt his guilt.

The hypocrites all
Stood and watched Rosie fall
As the trap door below her was sprung.
And each in his way
Will remember the day
That poor Rosie O'Grady was hung.

The Longbranch was closed
When her sins were exposed
And her doors were all boarded down tight.
Some folks will confide
They hear singing inside
When they listen intently at night.

No more do they roam,
The men all now stay home
With their wives all happy and cozy.
For they learned their lesson
And all stopped their messin'
Because of the death of poor Rosie.

It never does pay
If you wander away
To be with a woman who's shady.
You'll live with regret
If you ever forget
The Ballad of Rosie O'Grady.

The Coal Miner's Life

Michael R. Ritt
Huson, MT

"Son, Mr. Potter asked for the rent again today.
I turned him down. What could I say?
He's good enough about it though. He said
we could take another week. The bread
is on the table. I knew you'd be home soon.
You sit yourself down and I'll spoon
on the gravy. How goes your job?
Up on top of that little knob
of a hill lies your father; put
there dead from the dust and the soot
of the mine. I almost wish you hadn't gotten his berth
in that dark hole. Men should stay on top of the earth
and not go digging around inside of it for coal,
like so many ants around an ant hole.
But God knows we need the money you'll be gettin'.
Oh well. I suppose there's no need frettin'
about it. Your father's gone and you're
our only boy and I know I swore
I'd never see my son go down that mine,
but that was before we put your father in that pine

box and set him at ease atop that hill.
And us owing everyone a bill.
It sickens my heart to know you're down there
breathing the same poisoned air
that put your father on top of that little mound.
He worked his whole life inside the ground,
and now that he's gone that's where he'll lie.
Only this time he'll be starin' up at the sky.
How about some more gravy, son?
You want to go back to work lookin' like a skeleton?"

The Perfect Rose

Michael R. Ritt
Huson, MT

Today I saw a perfect rose
Without a single flaw.
Its petals glistened in the dew
Like ice before a thaw.

Its color was the deepest red
That I had ever seen.
I saw it growing in the rocks
So lonely and serene.

Its fragrance filled the evening air
And floated on the breeze.
It wafted ever heavenward
Ascending through the trees.

I asked the gardener how he came
To grow a perfect rose.
What fertilizers did he use?
And in what ratios?

He looked at me with knowing eyes
And gave a little smile.
"Look closer at the rose, my son,
And stare at it a while."

Then looking closer I beheld
What I'd not seen before.
It wasn't perfect after all
But little scars it bore.

In other places it looked crushed
And bleeding through the bruise.
And all at once I knew that its
Perfection was a ruse.

He said, "The bleeding that you see
Upon the rose's bloom,
Was caused by growing through the rocks,
But makes its sweet perfume.

It is the trials that we bear,
The rocky soil of life,
The pain and struggles we endure,
The heartache and the strife.

The people that would cause us pain,
The insults that we face,
That we forgive with tenderness,
With mercy and with grace.

The gardener uses all of these
To fertilize his rose.
And so with people, as with flowers,
That's how perfection grows."

Chasing Wheat

Steve Rose
Indianola, IA

I was not one of those boys
of my generation who dreamt
of running away with the circus
that came through towns
chasing county fairs,
trailing elephants and dancing
girls like cans on strings
on the heels of summer like dogs.

Instead I'd straddle bowlegged
my three-speed Schwinn and stare
at Highway 83 in July, watching combine
after combine, piggybacked on tractor
trailers—Peterbuilts and Macs,
Kenworths and Internationals
that smoked their way across
the North Platte River valley,
then rolling north over the Nebraska
Sandhills to Mission, South Dakota,

then Bismark that squatted
beneath the forty-ninth parallel.

That greasy diesel stench
called to my nose like a siren.
I imagined wearing scuffed boots,
metal toes staring out like owl eyes,
practicing my profanity
scooping beans from the can
with my fingers, sneaking gulps
of any Schlitz left unattended,
becoming the boy mascot
of that unholy crew,

easing Allis Chalmers thrashers
down from their mooring, watching
the blades churn through red
winter wheat, admiring the grain as
it shot up tubes and into
open wombs, ready
for birthing and banking.

The brood cows

Steve Rose
Indianola, IA

have been moved to the creek pasture.
Being Shorthorn, it was a simple feat.
They stand or lie still, almost ceramic,
tails limp, this spring's horse flies
yet larvae.

Their barreled bellies heave,
heavy with calf. One stub-tailed
piebald stands, tautens, drops offal
by the pound. Her calf will soon
follow.

They're pink in their rear parts,
labia stretching like the wings of a moth
still trapped in chrysalis.
A roan stands, slack-sided,
on a hill.

Above her, a white bull calf gambols,
ivory and pink like a plum blossom,

dancing on newfound legs, thinking
he's Christ.

Below the piebald cow strains,
ribs spreading like springs,
a stippled calf slides out,
anointed in her mother's oil,
then tongued dry. Her eyes are
ringed, one black, one brown:
the pasture jester.

If New Information Won't Stick

Marge Saiser
Lincoln, NE

My mother in her bed in assisted living
can't make the remote work
to get the channel she wants.
Maybe that blank spot lies ahead for me
where I won't remember the recent, will know
only what I knew as a child. If so, I'll have
the sound of the breeze through the corn
in its rows in the heat of August.
I'll know the iron taste of water from the pump,
how cold it was, splashing my face and arms.
I'll know the sad long grief of the mourning dove.
Waving seed heads of side-oats gramma
will stay with me and technology will
not. I'll be angry, as she is, and curse
when I can't put my finger on what I need to know,
but I'll have the two-note song of the killdeer
feigning a broken wing, flapping
to lure me away from its nest on the ground.

Looking for America

Marge Saiser
Lincoln, NE

I'm a first-timer at Janet's Cafe
and the half-dozen regulars are watching
me, the outsider, at my table alone.

Janet comes out of the kitchen, wiping her hands.
She tells me she slid the pork in and
slammed the oven door on it early this morning.

I like pork to roast slow, she tells me. Janet
apparently knows how to make dumplings,
and did today. I have lucked into a bonanza:

pork, mashed potatoes, kraut, corn, dumplings,
gravy over anything I want.
For balance Janet has placed a slice of bread,

rested it partly on the rim of the plate
and partly on the pork, and if
the bread soaks up a little gravy, isn't life good?

I am a stranger in a strange land
and was almost so foolish as to forgo the special
and ask for the grilled cheese, please.

What, you one of those vegetarians, Janet
might have said, but she says nothing of the kind,
rattling a big pitcher of ice and water

toward me, in case I want that
besides my Pepsi today. She's gone the easy route,
she says, going to Styrofoam plates,

makes it easier, she says, and who's to argue, because
when she sets that plate so solidly down before me
I feel less and less the interloper.

From out of town, aren't you, she says, and I am,
but I think, when she says Come back anytime,
that Yes, maybe I will.

Our Windows Were Single Pane

Marge Saiser
Lincoln, NE

No insulating layer, and so in winter
frost formed on the inside.
My fingernails scratched into the lacy

pattern, the curving fern-like leaves.
I pressed my warm palm
against that soft cold art. I melted

a peephole, blew breath on it,
scratched the aperture bigger.
Thin pane. On one side: Home and

a pot of soup on the stove. On the other:
the world and its curiosities.
Between home and adventure

I take up my post, where today again
there is so much to see, inner and outer,
from this frosted opening.

The Boogeyman

Maria I. Sanderson
Hamilton, NJ

The boogeyman is real
I know because
He came last night
And stole my dear tia

He left me a woman that staggers
Who looks and sounds like auntie
But this one is lost, frail and haggard

Gone is the person who laughed at my jokes
Gone is the workaholic, the fix it all
Who collected swirly color balls
And shopped in malls

Gone is the woman who used to cook
She's been replaced with one who's lost her checkbook

When she's not asleep in front of a screen
She fights windmills causing a scene

Looking for her missing keys
Her only joy now is a child's toy

Doctors are fooled by this new form
Medications refuse to resolve
And restore her back to norm
Why did you steal my aunt?
Boogeyman, I want her back

Looking Cool in School

Janet Sobczyk
Omaha, NE

Baggy blue jeans
cover skinny legs

new sneakers
support his need for speed
cushion fidgeting feet

gray unzipped hoodie
reveals black t-shirt with stark skull design

raised hood
conceals shaved haircut
provides security as well as warmth

dark sunglasses with scorpion logo
soothe sensitivity to light

black gloves with skeleton finger graphics
worn year-round, even indoors
hide eczema, prevent scratching

he skirts the crowds
finds quiet nooks
endures tactile irritations

tries to focus
struggles to learn
works to control explosive temper

today he succeeds
earns free time on laptop
settles into desk chair
with chin on hands, shaded eyes
appear engrossed with screen
soft snores betray his exhaustion.

If I Must Go

Valerie Lee Vierk
Ravenna, NE

If I must go, Lord,
And well I know I must someday,
Please let it not be in spring—
Glorious, rapturous spring
When life is bursting forth all over the land.

Oh, I don't want to leave your earth
When everything is so soft and lovely!
Not when the little lambs and foals and calves
Dot the newly greened landscape
And frolic so happily over it.

Not when the tulips and daffodils
Light up the walkways and gardens,
Nor when the robins are singing
Their enchanting spring songs
In the warm evenings
As I walk among them and drink in the soft air.

And no, I could never leave
When the blossoms are in bloom:
The apple, the pear, the cherry
And my favorite, the wild plums—
The darlings of the Nebraska spring,
Whose delicate fragrance wafts on the breeze.

No, Lord, don't make me go
When the blossoms fill the air!
If I smell them a hundred times
In an April day
It would never be enough.

If I must go, Lord, leave your beautiful earth,
Let it be in November
When the last golden leaf has fallen
The last southbound goose has flown
And the sky has turned to gray.

That is the only time I could go,
And even then reluctantly.
You will have to take me quickly
Before you send one of your gentle snowfalls
To cover the drab earth with the pure ermine.

The brief interlude between autumn and winter
Is the only time I could leave, if indeed I must,
And I will have to be far from here
When spring breaks again upon the land
Or I will surely want to return home again

As a lamb or a blossom or a swan
To revel in the spring.

Acknowledgments

The Nebraska Writers Guild would like to acknowledge the contributions of the following, without whom this collection would not exist. Volunteers make the success of the Guild and all its endeavors possible. Our deepest gratitude to everyone who gives their time in support of our organization and members.

Planning Committee: Wayne Anson, Charlene Neely, Kristin Burnett, Laura Madeline Wiseman, Cort Fernald, Charlene Pierce, Kim Sosin

Submissions Evaluators: Charles Peek, Kristin Burnett, Charlene Neely

Marketing Manager: Charlene Pierce

Communications Assistants: Kristin Burnett, Kim Sosin

Publication Consultant: Julie Haase

Editor: Julie Haase

Interior Design and Publishing: Infusionmedia, with a special thanks to Cris Trautner

We would also like to give a special shout-out to Wayne Anson, who has, as always, gone above and beyond to make this chapbook happen. Also, thank you to all those who submitted poems, whether they were selected for publication or not. Your creative spark is what this book is all about. Thank you for sharing your vision with us.

Index by Author

Anderson, Brad 1
Adkins, Lucy 3, 5
Anson, Wayne 7
Bean, Dan 8
Burnett, Kristin 10
Cain, Kathleen 12, 14, 16
Chelewski, Lynn 18
Egger, Christine 20
Faber, Rebecca 21, 23, 25
Fosbinder, Stephanie 27, 30, 32, 34, 36
Frolander, Pat 40, 41
Haase, Julie 42
Jacobs, Kathy 43, 45, 48
Joseph, Lori 51, 52, 54, 56
Luebbe, James 57, 59, 60, 62, 63, 65
Madison, Lynda 67, 68, 70
Marcusse, Jill 71, 73
Moran, Ricardo 74
Neely, Charlene 77, 79, 81
Pierce, Charlene 83, 85
Prettyman, Brandy 87
Ritt, Michael R. 89, 93, 95
Rose, Steve 98, 100

Saiser, Marge 102, 103, 105
Sanderson, Maria I. 106
Sobczyk, Janet 108
Vierk, Valerie Lee 110

Index by Title

Aloft 43
Ballad of Rosie O'Grady, The 89
Boogeyman, The 106
Bomb Cyclone 14
Broadway and 9th 74
brood cows, The 100
Canning Peaches 73
Chasing Wheat 98
Church Ladies 10
Coal Miner's Life, The 93
Creation of Birds, The 3
Cure, The 63
Dressmaker's Fingers, The 42
Em Counts 51
Evolution 87
Forty Days 25
Getting It Right 5
Gone 1
Gravity 71
Headstone Lost 18
How the Culture Crumbled 7
How to Create a Poet 77
If I Must Go 110

If New Information Won't Stick 102
In the After 34
In Your Shadow 83
Ironing 21
Last Mile, The 40
Looking Cool in School 108
Looking for America 103
Loose Change 48
Making Her Mark 79
Meadowlark Sings, The 52
Midnight on the Inca Trail 68
My Neighbor's Barn 59
My One and Only 85
Nebraskans 57
Night Approaches 20
Open Water 16
Our Sea of Tranquility 41
Our Windows Were Single Pane 105
Overcross 62
Perfect Rose, The 95
Platte River Sandbar 70
Pretty Bird 60

Progression of Trees, The 12
Tanzanian Bird 67
That Day at Whole Foods in
   Which I Put Myself Back
   Together 27
Things My Grandfather Left
   Me 65
Threshold 56
To the parents who sat behind
   me at my daughter's choir
   camp concert 36
Torrent 30
Tree of Knowledge 45
Tromso, Norway 23
Trusting in a Lie 8
Unfinished Dream 54
What Stuart Left Out 81
When the Night Cracks into a
   Fine Inaction 32

www.ingramcontent.com/pod-product-compliance
Lightning Source LLC
Chambersburg PA
CBHW020123130526
44591CB00032B/470